T0067833

An Open Book

Confessing Messy Faith amid Manicured Lawns

CINNAMON LINDAUERE

WESTBOW
P R E S S®
A DIVISION OF THOMAS NELSON
& ZONDERVAN

WestBow Press books may be ordered through booksellers or by contacting:

WestBow Press
A Division of Thomas Nelson & Zondervan
1663 Liberty Drive
Bloomington, IN 47403
www.westbowpress.com
1 (866) 928-1240

ISBN: 978-1-5127-9805-0 (sc)
ISBN: 978-1-5127-9806-7 (e)

Library of Congress Control Number: 2017912008

Print information available on the last page.

WestBow Press rev. date: 8/8/2017

Contents

Little Things

Do not despise these small beginnings, for the Lord
rejoices to see the work begin.
—Zechariah 4:10 (NLT)

Sometimes, it's the little things. When my baby cries at the hour she normally sleeps. When surprise fevers come on sunny days with prior plans. When my "perfect mommy" facade crumbles into, "Wait, is this just life now?" Little things, but they make me doubt. I doubt I'm a halfway decent mother. I doubt what I'm doing really matters. I doubt I even know what I'm doing most days.

Don't get me wrong; I always knew becoming a mother would mean being selfless. I thought I was generally selfless already, until I had less time, less money, and less attention paid to me. Every day still, I'm learning how selfish I can be, and it's hard. I mean, these are my kids and my husband; if there's anyone I want to pour my time out for, or pour my love into, or serve selflessly, these people are the ones. So when I find how narrow my limits are—the ever-finite failings of my love—I'm frustrated with me.

I think about how God didn't spare even His only beloved child. While I was yet His enemy, an unrepentant sinner, He poured His everything out for me.

Man, I want to be like that—right up until naptime. Then I want quiet. I want to sit alone—and usually think about me. So I get the baby to sleep, and I take the kids upstairs for quiet time, but the toddler trips on the first step and screams. The baby wakes up screaming. I kind of feel like screaming too. Little things.

Then I remember I've been loved by Jesus through my temper tantrums, which I still throw all too often. So this one moment I choose Him. I sit and hold my little one; I speak calming words to soothe her view of the world. I speak comfort and love. My older kids drape their arms around us both. The baby finds her quiet again, and slips back into sleep.

Sometimes it's the little things.

My husband and I have four daughters. We didn't intend to— well, not in the beginning. We thought we might have two or three children back to back, and then we'd stop so we could retire early. Within the first few years after our first daughter was born, it became clear I wasn't getting pregnant again—and then I did. Our first two came four years apart. Not quite the plan, but we are fairly flexible people. A few years later, I figured two was the magic number, and a couple of years after that, it was four. We were surprised to suddenly double our family, and we were also exhausted, pushed beyond our comfort zone, and blessed beyond our measure. People started saying things to me such as, "You know they've figured out what causes pregnancy now, right?"

I do know. In the immortal words (because I never let them die) of Joaquin Phoenix from the movie *Signs*, "It felt wrong not to swing."

When we went from two to four, life changed. I became concerned with the Peter Principle. I remember that well from the days I went to work in nice shoes and clean clothes. (It's true; before momhood, my work clothes started and stayed clean. I can barely picture it now.) According to the Peter Principle, everyone gets promoted to their level of incompetency. You succeed at your position through promotions until you get promoted to a position in which you can no longer succeed. Having two children spaced four years apart was smooth, clean, and generally orderly.

Having four kids at all ages is chaos.

Uh-oh. Did I pass my level of competency?

Is the house a mess? Often.

Do I still wear makeup? Wait, do I still own makeup?

Do I find snacks under the car seat I don't remember feeding to the kids?

Uh-oh.

Did the kids eat something nourishing today? Yeah, they were pretty well fed. Did they learn something valuable? Let's hope it sticks. Did they get a ton of love? Yes.

My daily assessments reflect my shifting priorities—or perhaps, my refined priorities. I think of each child—uniquely marvelous. My eldest is a wise old soul, quick with truth and wisdom, and she is full of insight beyond her years, always in the middle of a good book and always ready to be kind to those who need it. My six-year-old is quick-witted and clever, full of humor and creativity, and a natural-born storyteller with a deep well of a heart. My two-year-old, who is already as expressive as anyone else in the house, is a total class clown. She speaks in long sentences that none of us understand yet, which gives the impression she isn't a toddler—just a short foreigner learning our language and customs. She's quick to kiss anyone's boo-boos, though she has usually caused them. She bursts into giggles over the slightest insinuations of "butt burps" (a phrase my eldest coined in her early years). Our youngest, only five months old now, is the most agreeable baby we've had yet. She sleeps well, plays well, and watches us from the command center of her Exersaucer like she's always wondering just what kind of family she's joined. It's a fair question.

I watch in awe most days as their identities bloom. I watch them grow and take shape. Would I trade one of them for a cleaner, quieter house? That's a ridiculous question.

Would I trade my minivan for a tiny unicycle? That's easier to maintain.

It's also a lot less valuable.

The lives I've been gifted have more value than anything else ever entrusted to me. They're more valuable than any other enterprise I've ever undertaken. Everything else I do in my life can be undone by time. Any money I make will be spent by strangers long after I'm gone. Anything I build can crumble or be demolished—and will in time.

These four souls God formed in me, using my very flesh, are immortal. No matter how long eternity stretches, so will they. When I think God used material from my husband and me to form four distinct, unique human beings, it starts to look like a miracle. The Peter Principle starts to look like weaker priorities, or at the very least, the wrong Peter.

Maybe the Peter Principle I should be thinking about is closer to this:

"On this rock, I will build My church, and the gates of hell shall not prevail against it" (Matthew 16:18 ESV).

Because it's the little things God uses to build His great things.

CHAPTER 2

The Big Picture

Before the mountains were born or you brought
forth the whole world,
from everlasting to everlasting, you are God.
—Psalm 90:2 (NIV)

Calendars have changed a lot in the past few decades; they come prefilled now. By the time they hit the wall, all the best real estate is claimed. I always imagine them like the old dance cards and filling up before the band even starts playing. I don't know if it's our national culture or the world at large, but busyness has moved in next to godliness.

My husband and I are not tempted to busy schedules. We are in no way drawn to that lifestyle. We might be allergic to it. We chafe under inky calendars. We handle our schedules like Edward Scissorhands: oops, snip, oops, snip-snip. We cut free every moment we can. We value our family time. We love our "empty" days.

Even still, I find our family getting lost in the routine sometimes. So one day I decided we should all get away together.

I popped online and quickly found a cabin to rent for a weekend. Less than two hours from our house, it fell in our budget, and it was nestled right against a lake in the mountains. What really sealed the deal? It was also nestled in a dead zone, so no cell phones, no Wi-Fi, and no streaming masses of synthetic visual stimulation.

I discussed the idea with my husband, who jumped at the opportunity with a resounding "Sure." Our Friday came, and I packed everything we needed for our infant, our toddler, and the two kids. I threw together a couple of things for my husband and me too. When he got home from work, we wedged everything into our minivan. We knew we'd need to pick up groceries, so we found the grocery store nearest the cabin and plugged it into the GPS. We set out as one bouncing, happy family.

When the GPS allows for a two-hour drive, it really should offer to calculate the added time for each additional child. After gas and potty breaks—and pauses for carsickness—we arrived in town near sunset. We were not so bouncy. No problem. We were in the homestretch. Shopping for vacation foods buoyed our spirits as we anticipated the weekend ahead of us. The sky was dark as we loaded our spoils into the nooks and crannies between luggage and baby supplies. We fed everyone and diapered the little ones, who we assumed would soon be sleeping.

We put the cabin's address into the GPS. Hmm. Two identical options came up, miles apart. No matter; they were both on the same road. As we forged our way into the mountains, the night yielded a soft, consistent rain. Our infant, Calliope, refused to sleep. Her complaints gave way to screams that, in turn, pulled angry screams from our toddler, who truly wanted to sleep. I tried to speak comfort, if they could even hear me, as I kept driving through the dark, through the rain, and through the noise, looking for road signs or house numbers.

My husband and I tried to remember the name of the cabin, but every name we saw looked right and wrong at the same time.

My husband said the owner's directions were, "The house is about a mile after the road ends." What does that even mean? Ah, the lines disappeared from the road. Okay. I checked the odometer: one more mile, and this all gets better. The mile came, and went, but no house came with it. The screaming felt like it was getting worse, or maybe my nerves were getting worse. We passed the GPS destination with no destination, so I switched to the further address.

The pavement road turned to gravel, and the van began making noises like we were driving on rumble strips down the interstate. I felt every bolt shaking loose, and I also mean the ones in the van. In the dark rain, I saw only a few feet ahead of me in the headlights, so I drove slower than I wanted to, pressed forward in my seat, peering at every sign of habitation.

"Mom," my six-year-old croaked, "I feel really carsick."

It was raining, and there was no shoulder, so we asked her to hang in there and helped her with breathing exercises. Less than a mile, I figured, less than a mile. My eldest daughter told her sister to lay her head in her lap, tenderly taking care of her. God bless firstborns. The gravel road continued on, past the mile, and possibly forever. The babies kept screaming.

"I'm sorry," I whispered to my husband.

"What?"

"I'm sorry. This is all on me. I did this to our family. I did this. I'm so sorry."

He chuckled.

He *chuckled.*

"Tomorrow," he said, "when we're having fun, you'll be thanking *me* for this weekend."

Tomorrow? There was no tomorrow. Tomorrow was never going to come, because I'd booked us a cabin in the Twilight Zone. I wanted to be alone and unreachable with my family, surrounded by nature. Well, there we were on a never-ending road into the belly of earth with no cell reception, but plenty of dirt and rain and tree branches clasping around us like fingers closing into a fist. I've heard the road to hell is paved with good intentions, but it turns out it isn't paved; it is perpetually one mile ahead.

My six-year-old called out once, and then threw up where she lay. I pulled over as far as I could off the road. We pulled her out and cleaned what we could in the darkness and rain. We got back on the road again—the road I'd grown to hate, and soon the gravel gave way to dirt. After a mile or so, we saw the house. In the pitch dark, we recognized it. We recognized the name. I tried to stay on the circular driveway as best I could when pulling in, but the ground shone like a single sea of blackness in my headlights. Leaving everyone in the car, I felt along the porch railing until I found a door. I used my husband's phone as a lantern (it was good for little else here), and entered the code into the little box on the doorknob. No key ever looked so beautiful.

I opened the house, turned on lights, and helped unload the van. While I cleaned everyone up and prepared the bedrooms, my husband (the saint) cleaned the backseat. I put the little ones to sleep. We regrouped in the kitchen to put away the food and snack a little ourselves. We pulled out the board-game bag and sat with our oldest two children to laugh and play together before heading to bed.

Evening almost salvaged.

Sleep came fast and thick, but I awoke before the sun to care for our infant. When she drifted back to sleep, I brewed a pot of coffee and headed to the shower, eager to scrub off the road trip. Ugh. I forgot shampoo. Oh, and I forgot soap too. I briefly considered a weekend with no soap, then gently woke my husband, and told him I was heading back out to the store. I walked back through the darkness, climbed behind the wheel, saved my current location in the GPS, gritted my teeth, and pulled my tired van once more onto the road of nightmares.

Then the sun began rising.

The dark, thin tunnel of endless road widened into a tangle of forest. Trees, bushes, gentle hills, and lawns, even quaint cabins nestled off the road, all appeared in hazy beauty. Soon, great heights of green-painted mountains rose into the sky on all sides, flecked with shades from yellow to auburn to greet the coming season. Following the road, a bright river lapped and danced alongside me, with blinding peaks of light reflecting its mirth. Golden sunlight permeated everything, bathing every sight in beauty and wonder. I took gulps of it as it took my breath away.

In the dark, I hated this road because all I could see was the bit of road ahead of me, but now I could see so much more. It was too immense for me to see it all. Now I loved this road, this drive, even though I knew the road hadn't changed—just my ability to see.

I praised my God, the Maker of mountains.

When I got back, after a shower and a cup of coffee, I had an amazing weekend with my family.

I praised my God, the Maker of family.

I thanked my husband for the trip.

We smiled and kissed.

CHAPTER 3

Making a List

How do you know what your life will be like
tomorrow?
Your life is like the morning fog—it's here a little
while, then it's gone. What you ought to say is, "If the
Lord wants us to, we will live and do this or that."
—James 4:14–15 (NLT)

*T*he last job I held before giving birth to my first daughter was neither my most glamorous position nor my highest paid, but it might have been my favorite. It may not have been the highest-grossing job, but I was engrossed with it. Are you ready? I was the assistant store manager at a Blockbuster Video store.

That's right: a job with a real future.

For those who remember Blockbuster stores, or video stores in general, their concept was simple. The entire shop consisted of one room, a backroom, a bathroom, and a front counter. In the one great room, physical copies of DVDs lined every surface, and yes, some VHS tapes still, too. We arranged impulse buys near the front counter for last-minute stock-ups of sodas, popcorn, and lots of candy. As an employee, I received five free rentals a week.

Believe it or not, that wasn't what I loved most. I'd never been an adamant movie junkie before those days. I liked going to the theater; I liked the experience and the company. I just never thought to watch at home. My own TV remained unplugged until a visitor tried to "fix" it. While working at Blockbuster, I played some pretty fast catch-up with my movie knowledge. I didn't always mind that, but it wasn't what I loved.

I loved the paperwork. Monday mornings were my favorite because there was so much paperwork. I came in early, unlocked the door, turned off the alarm, and locked myself back inside. The store lay dim and quiet as I tiptoed to the back room to print my daily tasks.

I did tiptoe. I could have lumbered. I was alone in the store for the next hour or so, but I tiptoed through as though a heavy footfall might wake the rows of titles sleeping like perched owls on every side. I gathered my paperwork and nestled back behind the front counter.

I had a checklist to complete.

I sorted, stapled, and filed. I counted tills, twice, and prepared deposits, deposit slips, reports, and tracking sheets. After a quick trip to the bank, I returned, tucked my clipboard in an arm, and began moving through my morning tasks. I loved those columns of empty boxes next to each task: each one awaiting my initials. I loved preparing that list and completing each task so I could turn it in to my smiling manager. I even loved making the outgoing calls. Anyone who knows me should be shocked to hear that, but I did. I loved it because no one else in the store would do it, but if I did, all the boxes got checked.

I loved the order of the store: a place for everything, and everything in its place. I always paused to face merchandise, to properly space product, and process all returns promptly. I kept my store neat, stocked, and dressed to impress. When people joined me in the store, employees and sometimes even customers, I was a good manager: firm but fair, friendly, and knowledgeable. I practiced being kind to everyone. I possessed the vague feeling I could run a home with the same precision I ran my store. I wasn't worried.

As I write, I'm sitting in our library/schoolroom. The homemade shelves are slightly crooked—I can see it now that they're in place. Books are lining them neatly, and crammed on top, and stacked on the floor beside. Someday soon, I plan to make bigger, nicer shelves. On the floor in front of me, clean hand towels have been strewn by my toddler, after I folded them but before I put them away. A Dr. Seuss book is laid open, surrounded by primary-colored toddler toys. A half-finished art project explains the crayons speckling the floor; I just put them all away yesterday. There's a singing puppy, the kind you switch off every time you pass it, smiling at me with a frozen expression. Half-melted, brightly colored balloons, leftovers from a recent birthday, tremble with each draft, quietly begging me to put them out of their misery. Half of them have faces drawn on them, and it's true, once you name them, they're yours forever.

I look around me, and I wonder if I undervalued the employees paid to keep my store tidy. I bet they should have been paid more. I chuckle at my younger self for comparing video-store apples to my current-day oranges. It took years and multiple children for me to get here today, to this scene ahead of me, and maybe that was too long.

When I changed jobs from assistant store manager to assistant home manager, I didn't account for the change in substance that came with it. I still started my day with checklists, affixed with magnets to the fridge, and I worked for each check mark. I waited for my husband to come home from work for my performance evaluations: my gold stars. I kept quiet the nagging fear that I wasn't meant for motherhood because it wasn't as fulfilling as I expected. I didn't question where I was looking for that fulfillment.

After all, I was getting my items crossed off. I was a great employee.

Through the years, those checklists morphed and shifted, changing in form, but they remained. I grew discontent listing chores like "laundry" and "dishes," because I always did them, but they were never done. I began pushing myself to complete something, anything, that wouldn't make the expected daily list. Eventually, that's all that went on the list. As we had more kids, I began calling it my wish list. I stopped considering myself a great employee, or housekeeper, or wife, or mother.

One day, far too recently, I poised my pen between a blank page and my first cup of coffee and decided to write a new list, a "reverse list," as I called it. Throughout the day, until my husband arrived home (because that's when I clock out, right? That's another chapter—or book), I wrote down whatever I did. It's so simple that I'm hard-pressed to find another way to explain it. As I did anything, I wrote the activity on the list.

To my shock, I filled pages. Most of them weren't complex tasks, but I was completing them, so they went on the list. That afternoon I stopped to look over the list, and I saw something remarkable. It wasn't how busy I stayed, although I did stay busy. It wasn't how many items were on my list, although there were more than expected.

I saw my kids.

My precious children are so far more complex than the simplicity of checklists allows. Each of my children is in a different stage, with different needs. I'd been so busy focusing on the *what* of each day that I diminished the importance of the *who*. Anything I completed only carried importance if it added value to the *who*.

I look now into the faces of the balloons on the floor. Yup, I look right into their Sharpie faces. They cannot last. Their time was always intended to be brief, but the laughter they give my family, the impromptu balloon battles staged on the kitchen floor, these echo into eternity.

My new daily checklists are shorter now, and I love each repetition. They look something like this:

<u>Tuesday</u>
God
John (my husband)
Azalea Grace
November Verity
Rhiannon Jubilee
Calliope Hope

My neighbors?
My friends?
My church?

My enemies?

Reverse Checklist

<u>4:00 a.m.–5:00 a.m.</u>
Took care of Calliope

<u>7:00 a.m.–7:30 a.m.</u>
Washed laundry
Got coffee and bagel
Listened to Bible (1 Corinthians)
Folded laundry

<u>8:00 a.m.</u>
Fed girls
Got Rhiannon
Changed diapers

<u>8:20 a.m.</u>
Folded laundry

<u>8:30 a.m.</u>
Stripped November, put in shower
Put shower slip-guards in place
Stripped bedding
Collected laundry from upstairs

<u>9:00 a.m.</u>
Washed laundry
Folded laundry
Put out candles
Fed Calliope
Changed and dressed Calliope

<u>9:15 a.m.</u>
Folded laundry
Microwaved coffee

Fed Rhiannon again
Found charger, plugged in iPad
Folded laundry

9:30 a.m.
Refilled coffee
Folded laundry

9:35 a.m.
Resolved fight upstairs
Changed Rhiannon's diaper
Folded laundry

9:40 a.m.
Fed November and Rhiannon
Rotated/washed laundry
Found box for gift in basement
Folded laundry

10:00 a.m.
Didn't treat Rhiannon harshly for waking Calliope
Didn't treat November harshly for dropping every single metal
piece of the toaster trays, one by one on the floor, after I got
Calliope calm again
Microwaved coffee (started feeling hungry)
Folded laundry
Fed Calliope

10:10 a.m.
Made sure bathroom was dry after showers
Dried floor/turned fan back on (why do they always turn off
the fan?)
Collected laundry

Searched for Rhiannon's missing banana
    Found missing waffle and bagel instead
Folded laundry

<u>10:30 a.m.</u>
Took chicken to sink to thaw
Rotated laundry
Stopped kids from arguing
    Got them back on track
Changed Azalea's sheets/made bed
Replaced towels in bathroom
Collected more laundry

<u>10:45 a.m.</u>
Cleaned up after breakfast
Microwaved coffee
Folded laundry

<u>11:00 a.m.</u>
Refilled coffee—end of pot
Folded laundry
Picked up strewn diapers—Rhiannon was presumably attempting to plant diaper trees all inside our house: a remarkable child!
Gave Rhiannon laundry hamper rides

<u>11:10 a.m.</u>
Got Calliope
Cleaned up November's milk (which Rhiannon used to water the house: remarkable!)
Changed Calliope's diaper
Picked up puzzle pieces Rhiannon scattered over floor and under table

Brought November in to finish destroying assembled puzzle (as promised)
Put away (hopefully all of) puzzle—pulled out next puzzle box

11:18 a.m.
Fished chewed-up puzzle pieces from Rhiannon's mouth
Threw away puzzle
Got Rhiannon sippy cup
Cleaned Calliope spit-up from Exersaucer
Rotated laundry
Got Rhiannon off Calliope
Put Calliope's jacket back on
Folded laundry
Got Rhiannon off computer/turned off monitor, moved chair
Put Calliope in swing
Took phone away from Rhiannon

11:28 a.m.
Carried Rhiannon with me upstairs to check on older girls
They're so sorry
Got them back on track/went back downstairs
Rhiannon screamed when I put her down/ Calliope started screaming too

11:30 a.m.
Made Calliope's bottle—started considering lunch options
Loved the chorus of tears—Merry Christmas to all
Gave Calliope her bottle—figured out lunch
Took bottle from Rhiannon
Wiped clean and returned to Calliope
Gave Rhiannon Clementines
Put water on for mac 'n' cheese
Put out veggies (and ranch today)
Gathered girls

Moved Calliope to Exersaucer
Rinsed sticky green beans (gross) and bowled
Rinsed carrots and bowled
Held back green beans (too gross)
Made pasta
Rhiannon threw carrot across room—hit the button on the
food scale, which beeped loudly
 All the kids cheered for Rhiannon
Stopped Rhiannon from throwing carrots
Stopped Rhiannon from throwing celery instead
Made note to make time for a super private, personal question
Azalea wants to discuss
Cleaned up odd water all over counter (??)—check for leak
Due to fussing, added Calliope to my hip
Cleaned the milk soup-bowl that was Rhiannon's tray
Ate broad array of scattered vegetables bearing Rhiannon's
dental marks
Put away rest of veggies
Sent November up with folded laundry
Had a great private conversation with Azalea
Gave Calliope bottle
Cleaned and redressed Rhiannon

12:15 p.m.
Got this list back from Rhiannon
Sent kids upstairs for play break
Rotated laundry
Cleaned out old containers from fridge
Put away mac 'n' cheese

12:30 p.m.
Cleaned dishes, soaked some
Put chicken in fridge
Changed Calliope's diaper on couch

Cleaned spit-up off couch
Put Calliope in butterfly seat by me
Sent Rhiannon back upstairs—instructed older kids to play
with her
Microwaved coffee
Folded laundry
> Finally got chocolate stain from Azalea's white shirt!
Moved Calliope around looking for her happy place

12:45 p.m.
Answered doorbell—someone looking for neighbors
Cleaned space on shoe shelf for basket for neighbors
> Found book and mugs to return to neighbors, added
to pile
Kicked latest wave of laundry into laundry room
Sent kids back upstairs
Calmed Calliope—even tried a pacifier—then a rattle
Folded laundry (dyed load pink)
Responded to shouting upstairs
Returned to sit and rock a despondent Calliope

1:15 p.m.
Put calm Calliope in swing to get her to cry again
Finished load of laundry
Moved trash can so mailman could get to box
Went upstairs to check on kids and put Rhiannon down to nap
> Took Azalea's folded laundry with me
Brushed, changed, read, and sang to Rhiannon
Calliope was quiet, checked quickly on older girls before going
downstairs
Calliope fell asleep!

1:30 p.m.
Quiet time!
Seriously considered eating tons of Ramen noodles
    Twenty minutes left until next load of laundry
Found cold coffee cleverly hidden in microwave
Never found banana—John will, with his toes

2:00 p.m.
Neighbors returned home—delivered items to them
Calliope—diaper, bottle, etc.
Donnie came, collected mail
Opened package, hid gift
Rotated laundry
Folded laundry—finished load
Microwaved coffee

2:30 p.m.
Calliope slept
Played app

2:57 p.m.
John got home!
Took shower

CHAPTER 4

Oh Captain, My Captain

Obey your leaders and submit to them, for they are
keeping watch over your souls,
as those who will have to give an account.
Let them do this with joy and not with groaning,
for that would be of no advantage to you.
—Hebrews 13:17 (ESV)

Today is my husband's birthday. He's turning thirty-eight, or, as we're calling it, "thirty-great!" It seems fitting I write this chapter today, and I pray my honesty will honor him.

In the beginning of our marriage, I always felt alone. I felt like I'd found myself in the middle of the vast ocean in nothing but a tiny rowboat. I wanted desperately for my husband to get in the boat with me. I was sad, confused, and resentful. The waves of life came one after another, choppy, constant, spreading relentlessly in every direction, and he was leaving me alone in my little rowboat to face it unsupported.

My eldest daughter began changing my ability to see things from a different perspective. Discovering I was with child found us with jokes as well. My husband and I discovered endless fodder in the potential future. We joked about all the unorthodox ways we would raise our unfortunate offspring. We enjoyed streams of concocted scenarios featuring our off-the-cuff approaches. We laughed and laughed. Oh, how we laughed.

Then I gave birth, and nothing was ever funny again.

I hope that's an exaggeration, but I can't swear to it. Overnight, my world became one long, intense struggle. I worried about her. I worried about her feedings, her weight, how many diapers she filled, how many hours she slept, her skin tone, her brain development, her every development. I slept very little, and I stressed very much. Life went from being one big joke to one big business, and I was the micromanager.

As she grew, I expanded my territory into her emotional well-being. I insinuated myself between her and every attempt by my husband to discipline her. My husband isn't given to anger, but she was my ward, and I had to protect her from any harsh words. I became the advocate everyone, even my husband, had to go through to interact with her. I shielded her from every unpleasantry I could, even the necessary ones.

Soon I was no longer running things: my toddler was. Somehow, with all her life experience, life still wasn't running smoothly. It didn't make sense. She started throwing full-blown temper tantrums for things even she didn't care about. I resented my husband more, ever so subtly, for leaving me in the rowboat with a "strong-willed child" to parent alone. I felt that if he could just handle her the right way—my way—without ever sounding harsh or authoritative, I could trust him with her. I could take breaks. My stress level grew, and I couldn't let any of it out on my little angel, so it festered or leaked out at my husband.

Then one day my daughter cracked a smile in my direction. She smiled at me.

In a moment when everything seemed right with the world, my daughter smiled. Her little smirk curled, half-hidden, half-beaming, with the quiet exultation of knowing she'd been clever, but not knowing if anyone else saw it.

But I saw it. I'd seen it before. It was her father's smile. It suddenly struck me that she didn't belong to me. She wasn't mine alone. Half of her, and maybe even the best half, wasn't made out of me. She was, down to her DNA, half his. She belonged to him too. He owned equal rights, an equal say, in how she should be reared.

After that, I pulled back and let him father as he saw fit. I remember so clearly restraining my urge to interfere the first time he disciplined her. To my surprise, what I saw as harsh at first melted into tender. He was her father and expected her to listen, but she was his little girl, and he adored her.

The temper tantrums dwindled away. I saw his way was far better for us all. Everyone was happier, and adults ran the household again. My daughter was happier. She was calmer and started seeing how other people felt in different situations. She started truly hearing me, and our time together became even more precious. She loved her father all the more.

I came on board quickly after that and never looked back. I learned to trust my husband's instincts and then to rely on them.

So how did this situation begin a change in my marital rowboat analogy?

I'm glad you asked.

When I felt alone as a parent, it was because *my husband wouldn't get into the boat with me.* I didn't see he was steering a much larger ship. From his position, he could see waves even farther in the distance than my little rowboat view allowed. What was true for us as parents is infinitely truer for us as husband and wife.

Ephesians 5:23 says, "For a husband is the head of his wife as Christ is the head of the church. He is the Savior of his body, the church" (NLT). My husband is my leader. He doesn't lead as I would because he isn't me, but he is leading as he is designed. His leadership isn't a role he has to earn or an activity he may do or may not do. No matter where we are as a couple, his position never changes. My critique of his performance, or my undermining or denying his leadership, never changes his position on the ship. As long as we are married, his hand is on the helm, whether he even wants it there or not.

All men are different. Some are assertive, energetic, and others, like my husband, are more quiet and passive. When I married my husband, I promised to love, honor, and obey, as is right I should. Asking him to be something he is not breaks all of those vows. His form of leadership will look as unique as he does. My role as his wife isn't to reprimand or bemoan who he isn't, but to support who he is. My job on the ship is to see that everyone recognizes his role as captain, and to create an environment in which he can lead, in his own unique way, to the utmost of his potential.

To wear out the rowboat/ship metaphor, there are a few other observations I've made through the years:

1. The longer I spend in my rowboat, the farther I drift from the ship.
2. Rowboats aren't designed to weather storms or cross the ocean of time, but a good ship (or marriage relationship) is a magnificent vessel crafted for just such a purpose.
3. Rowboats are a poor way to carry passengers and cargo, which makes rowboat parenting difficult at best.

These observations may sound preachy, but if so, I'm preaching to myself. Even after all I've seen, all I've learned, and all I've experienced, I still climb inside that stinking rowboat too often.

I've tried to destroy it or release it, but I find it intact again every time I feel like a jaunt. So I named it.

I named it, so every time I climb aboard and sit inside, everyone can see—*I* can see—what it really is. Around the prow, in big, bold letters, I painted, "MY FOOLISH PRIDE."

There is a practical note I must add. As I write this, my husband is not yet a believer. There are a few occasions where he may steer our family in directions we were not meant to travel. Those are the difficult times when I recognize his authority most clearly, but I must recognize its limitations also. Those are the times I must try to assist him as navigator.

My husband's authority as captain is given to him by God, but the ship itself also belongs to God. If my husband takes the vessel too far off course, God Himself will intervene. If I see our course veering outside of God's direction, I must go to my husband in quiet strength and let him know I cannot go where we are headed.

This is no small thing. First, *I must pray.* I must seek wisdom from God, which He liberally lavishes on those who ask. I must not make into moral issues things that are not. I must not expect my husband to delight in the things of God. I must love my husband more than I love myself by recognizing his full value and appealing to him in humility, in all grace and truth. I must love God more than I love my husband by saying with my life and actions, "I will have no other gods before You." I must love God with all my heart, mind, and strength, and also love my husband as myself.

I must love my husband, but not out past the breakers of a Spirit-driven conscience, "just as Sarah obeyed Abraham, calling him lord. And you are her children, *if you do good* [emphasis mine] and do not fear anything that is frightening" (1 Peter 3:6 ESV).

CHAPTER 5

The Good Life

This is My commandment, that you love one
another, just as I have loved you.
Greater love has no one than this, that one lay down
his life for his friends.
—John 15:12–13 (NASB)

*B*elieve it or not, I have a life. I have interests and hobbies. I have deep friendships, friends with whom I discuss deep things, weighty things, eternal things. I read and write and dream and plan and hope. I am human, in all the intricate complexities inherent to the condition. I refer to the sum of every detail of my unique condition, whether grand or mundane, as, "my life."

I remember reading the above verse as a child, the laying down your life for your friend, and thinking the idea was terribly romantic. I cannot say now what was essentially *romantic* about it, but that's the way it struck me. Dying for someone made them valuable. It meant that even all the details of a life weren't as valuable as the immortal identity a life contains. It meant imitating Jesus, the greatest expression of human life that ever existed. I loved—I was in love— with the idea of giving a gift few would dare give and none could take back.

Life comes to us in sequential moments. The only tools we have to master them are those gifted or garnered in the moments preceding them. I cannot say, in the height of my romantic fervor, if given the opportunity to die for a friend, I wouldn't have balked. I would probably balk at it still. There are reasons a person "will hardly die for a righteous man; though perhaps for the good man someone would dare even to die" (Romans 5:7 NASB).

Before I'm accused of being morbid, let me get to the point. In Luke it says, "If you are faithful in little things, you will be faithful in large ones" (Luke 16:10 NLT). I have found this to be, across the board, unceasingly true. My macrocosm mirrors my microcosm. If then I desire in the macrocosm to be someone who lays down her life for her friend, what is the shadow, the counterpart, in my microcosm?

Perhaps because I'm a literal person, I've found the answer in the term "lay down." I must lay down, or set down, my life for those in my life. I must set aside my hobbies, hopes, dreams, and plans for the people whose lives God has woven into my own. I didn't know as a little girl, dreaming of the grand, romantic gesture and thinking how rarely the opportunity presents itself, just how ample my opportunities would become.

Motherhood is a series of interrupted tasks. I feel like I've heard that somewhere. Maybe I have, or maybe it's so true it resounds like a cliché. Motherhood is one task that is comprised of a string of innumerable interrupted tasks. I spoke around this when I talked of checklists. Motherhood is full of hot cups of coffee growing cold while you attend to skinned knees. Motherhood is full of dinners simmering too long while you separate squabbling children, while you teach young souls to value people over things, and while you equip tender little moments for the larger ones to come.

Motherhood is a microcosm of improvised decisions that

ripple into the macrocosm of civilizations and cultures and the very timeline of humankind. Empires are laid or erode in the single bricks of a mother's snap decisions. This may sound grandiose, but it is so simple. Civilizations are built by people, and people are built by their parents. Children grow into adults, and as they grow, they learn what's important by what we show them is important. Will we set down our desires, our tasks, our short-term (or long-term) ambitions to invest in humanity entire? Will we lay down our lives, our moments here, for our children?

Sometimes I do.

Sometimes I drop everything to wipe tears, or soothe inexperienced nerves, or calm the fears of a tiny child in a world so much larger than that child is. Sometimes I put down whatever I'm doing to snuggle with someone who feels alone among a vast population. Sometimes I do it for my husband too. I cancel or reschedule plans because he seems to need some time with me, or some quiet time with himself. Sometimes I try to do those dirty jobs he always does, though we both know they bring no joy, such as taking out the trash or scrubbing dirty dishes. Sometimes I respond immediately to a crying baby or that sudden smell of a foul diaper so that he can have one more uninterrupted moment.

Sometimes I do these things, but too often I don't. Too often I'm concerned with my life, my desires, and my moments. Too often I am not concerned with laying down my life in the same humble service my Maker laid down His. I don't want to set it down; I want to hold it tightly with two fistfuls of white knuckles.

When I look back on the child I was, dreaming romantic dreams of dying for someone, I think what I liked most about the idea was that it seemed *easy*. One moment, one decision, one right turn of fate, and I've given the greatest gift possible. In one act alone, I become a saint worthy of veneration. In one decision, one gesture, I become a hero. In short, the idea of laying down my life was still all about me.

What I've learned in my adulthood is that rarely do I make a big decision that stands in stark contrast to all the small decisions that preceded it. If my life is only about me, certainly my death will follow suit. My legacy will be as short and limited as my own arm span, my own memory.

I wasn't formed as a center of gravity, and the world knows it. The world knows nothing revolves around me, so maybe I should know it too. How small my universe is when it revolves around me. How large it grows when it expands to include all those with whom I come into contact. Everyone is unique and precious and valuable because they are made in the image of the most unique, most precious, most valuable God. Each soul reflects some facet of His divine nature. Everyone has a special purpose in life, and that purpose is woven into the people God has given them. Just as Jesus prayed that He not lose one of those His Father gave Him, so also I pray that I see and love and lay down my life every day for every soul He's given to me to see, to love, and to serve.

Because the truth is, this is how I am designed to live to the fullest. If I spend my life on me, I multiply my stress. I build my expectations into high towers the circumstance of life cannot scale. I allow my expectations to draw divisions between myself and those I love. My life, focused on my needs, is a grumbling, shallow existence. But when I lay down my life, I find it.

We are designed for relationship, for love, and for each other. When I lay down my personal desires and expectations to engage in the life of someone else, I find that an even deeper desire in my soul is met. Self-sacrifice can often be the highest form of self-service. In laying down my life, I am picking up my calling. In laying down my life, I am fulfilling my design. My life suffers when I focus all my energies on me, but when I lay it down, I find the good life.

I find life abundant.

Dearest heavenly Father,

I am selfish. I am weak. I am myopic. You are sacrificially

selfless. You see it all and are strong enough to intervene. Help me today to see You in those around me, and to mirror You in the tiny moments that become our whole lives.

Thank You that while we were Your enemies, You laid down Your life, Your breath, and Your moments, for us. Thank You for being so grand the heavens cannot contain You, and yet You inhabit the confines of our small planet, and the even smaller confines of human skin and bone.

Thank You for caring enough about us to become less for us. Help me care enough about You to become more like You. Teach me how to lay down my life for Your friends. Lead me on the path to the good life: a life devoted to You. I love You; teach me to love You more. Teach me to love Yours.

Amen.

CHAPTER 6

Everyday Counts

Therefore be careful how you walk, not as unwise
men but as wise,
making the most of your time, because the days are
evil.
—Ephesians 5:15–16 (NASB)

*I*began my morning before the sun today. I've been doing that
a lot lately, to write this book. After getting my infant changed
and fed, she settles back in for a few hours. I sneak out to my porch
to read my daily devotionals on my YouVersion app. It's cold lately,
and I give each hand a turn wrapping around my hot coffee mug
before it grows cold too. The air bites my fingers and toes, but the
discomfort of it invigorates me; it helps me think.

My first devotional today, called "Spiritual Laws of
Progression," began with a reading titled the same as this chapter,
"Everyday Counts." It was a typo. The author was trying to say that
"every single day" counts. Every day means each day. Every day
refers to ongoing segments of time, but everyday has a different
nuance. Everyday (often an adjective) describes the substance of

that time. The everyday is that which is repetitive, commonplace, or mundane. The everyday things in life are unremarkable by their definition.

I love words. These little things catch my attention. I've made the same off keystrokes, and many times found hidden depths in the slip. Today this little typo struck me, got me thinking, "Do I live my *everyday* to the fullest?" Do I make the most out of diapers, or dishes, or laundry? Is that even possible?

I chewed on that as I moved to the next devotional, "Shaken," to complete the final reading. "Shaken" is a devotional based on the book written by Tim Tebow, the former football player. I have a confession to make: I picked the devotional after a quick sample, and only afterwards realized with grimace it was written by a sports personality. I expected the devotional to devolve into a rehash of glory days glossed over with thin spiritual application. I know the full depth of the prideful sin contained in that sentence. I am truly confessing.

In every respect, I was wrong. Mr. Tebow's devotional was concise, insightful, and wildly applicable to my own life. I was sad to reach the end of it, and humbled by what it exposed in me. The final day's reading discussed how we are each fearfully and wonderfully made. He asked his readers these two questions in closing:

1. What makes you different, special, unique?
2. How can you more fully live out the way God made you?

So I find myself ruminating on how I can embrace my unique design to live my everyday to the fullest divine potential, but I'm still pretty sure I'm going to drag myself through some chores today. I can't picture myself breaking into the hallelujah chorus when I discover loads of extra laundry to sort, wash, dry, fold, and put away. (The last step is always the most difficult for me.)

The reason I've shared these devotionals is because, like so many before them, they've come with the right words at the right time for me. You see, I've always known I would write this chapter. I've been dreading it. What I'm writing about is one of my weakest areas as a wife and mother. To pretend to offer guidance in the everyday ins and outs of my job feels like the blind leading the blind. I'm not a great housekeeper, but I'm better than I used to be. I'm only offering here what helps me grow in this area, but always bear in mind that I am woefully inadequate myself. I'm learning. I'm slowly shedding my blindness.

I call it blindness because I think my flaws in this area come from an inability to see. I have viewed daily tasks as the never-ending monotony of obligation: jobs I'm always doing but are never done. Like the dream Pharaoh recounts to Joseph: the lean cows of mundane activity swallow the fat cows of time, of potential, of substance: the lesser always feeding on the greater.

When I read of the Proverbs 31 woman, she has something vital I lack. I'm not speaking of her diligence, her skills, her personal business, though I lack these things too. She has vision. She has forward-thinking, and an eye to tomorrow. Here's a woman who looks at where her family is and also sees where they can be, then she acts. It isn't about keeping up with the Joneses. She sees the value of her husband, her household, and seeks to strengthen and increase it.

I will never love cleaning the bathroom, but I may learn to love the sense of satisfaction that comes with being a good steward of the bathroom. It seems like a never-ending task, an endless chore, but it isn't. Changing diapers seems endless, but diapers give way to toys, which give way to books, which give way to pictures on the memory wall of days I cannot relive, and *days I wish I could.*

As you may have already gathered, I'm not a sports fan. When I see an arena packed with cheering fans, I see a colosseum of people gawking at gladiators, living vicarious lives, feeling like warriors in ways they are not, and perhaps substituting the usurped elation for seeking out the ways they may yet be warriors. I don't enjoy sporting events, but I love playing sports. I love individuals coming together, practicing diligence and self-sacrifice, so the team as a whole can excel. I don't watch sporting events, but I love sports movies. *Rudy, Hoosiers, 42, Miracle, Rocky*: honestly this list will grow too long. I can't think of a sports movie I haven't loved.

However, the art of these movies lies entirely in the montage. One good, heart-thumping, adrenaline-producing song set to multiple clips of hard work all spliced together to denote the passage of time, and, abracadabra, zeroes are heroes.

We fast-forward the everyday struggles. We skip through the very part of the movie that changes the outcome of the movie, and rightly so. If we viewed the striving in real time, the small victories and failures, the sore muscles and raw nerves, we would need a broader range of musical accompaniment. If we watched every day of effort, endeavoring, tearing down only to build back up, quitting only to begin again, the gradual transformations, the movie would seem repetitive and endless.

I think we watch these movies to remind ourselves that goals, even seemingly impossible goals, can be reached through hard work and perseverance. (Teamwork is also invaluable where available.) What the Proverbs 31 woman had, and I lack, might just be a goal.

What is my goal for my household?

Every moment, every chore, every decision I make, is building my montage. Right now, I'm writing my future in tiny pieces, but every piece matters. Every small word is part of the larger story. Every moment matters. What do I want my montage to look like? Where do I want my montage to end?

I want my home to be a pleasing reflection of my family, a place of order and kindness and joy. I want my husband to be respected on account of me, and to have pride in finding me for a wife. I want my children to learn the value of discipline and structure, but also live their lives from a secure place of overwhelming love and grace.

I want my family to be familiar with giving, and serving. I want my family to be pleasing to God.

I'm still learning to refine my desires into goals. I'm learning to build my own exciting montage as I pursue those goals.

CHAPTER 7

My Next Wedding

I am overwhelmed with joy in the Lord my God!
For He has dressed me with the clothing of salvation
and draped me in a robe of righteousness.
I am like a bridegroom dressed for his wedding, or a
bride in her jewels.
—Isaiah 61:10 (NLT)

I was engaged once before I met my husband. Obviously, it didn't work out. As our relationship progressed, I think I knew in the depths of me it shouldn't be, but I chose to believe with the rest of me that it would all work out somehow.

As the day drew nearer for us to marry, an endless stream of preparatory tasks came nearer too. We picked venues. We hired a photographer. We went to look at wedding dresses. I remember looking for wedding dresses in particular. I, and a few other ladies, went to a posh boutique for all things wedding. Past the front counter lined with sample invitations, and the shelves of every conceivable pastel accessory, we passed into a rear antechamber. The back wall was hollowed out and filled to capacity with varying shades of crisp, white dresses. Endless yards of satin, silk, and tulle, tucked intimately cheek-to-cheek, should have resembled a row of white gardenias and roses. It was probably designed to look such. To my view, it may as well have been a row of bared white teeth. I remember feeling I was drowning in a great, white ocean. Either the room kept swirling, or I did, but everything spun on its own axis. Panic gripped me. With every passing moment I cared less for my need of a dress, or my upcoming wedding, or even the impression I would make on the ladies attending me, whether guests or employees; I just wanted out of there. I wanted to leave it behind and push it away.

I think the dress made it real. I think the dress exposed what I lacked. I thought I was ready to marry him. If the wedding custom entailed nothing more than swinging by a lawyer's office on a Tuesday afternoon and signing a contract, we would have been married already. Thankfully, weddings involve so much more.

Why is that? A marriage commitment should be a rational one. It should be made soberly, with open eyes and sound judgment. At that point, the idea of sitting with a lawyer and hashing out the goals, expectations, and limitations of our union would've probably sounded delicious to me. And so it was good I didn't marry then. I didn't see the full value of the wedding ceremony, because I couldn't yet see the full value of marriage. I wasn't ready to buy the dress, because I wasn't ready to delight in the groom.

In many ways, sadly, this experience correlates to my Christian life. The Bible often refers to the church as the bride of Christ. In some mysterious way, we will be His bride. For years, I handled my faith as I handled my first engagement: preparations were obligations. Obedience to God was about fulfilling the required and expected details that I knew I *should* do but I didn't necessarily desire to do. I wanted to be a good bride eventually, but I wasn't eager for the day. In many ways I resembled the words of Jeremiah:

Oh my people, listen to the words of the Lord!

Have I been a desert to Israel? Have I been a land of
darkness?
Why then do my people say, "At last! We are free from
God! We don't need Him anymore!"
Does a young woman forget her jewelry, or a bride her
wedding dress?
Yet for years on end my people have forgotten me.
(Jeremiah 2:31–32 NLT)

In my heart, the day deferred might not come. I put off
preparing my heart for my heavenly Groom. I postponed
obedience and forgot about my wedding dress.

I'm glad to say my next engagement went better than my first.
We were eager for the day. More invitations meant more witnesses
to share in our celebration, to help us in our commitment, and
to hold us accountable. A photographer meant more moments
captured, treasured, and remembered. Flowers, pew bows,
accessories, attendants, and a host of other details all set the day
apart as distinctive and special. Honoring our parents in the
ceremony involved our pasts with our future, establishing our
decision as a lifetime commitment. Plotting out our ceremony
and laying out our bulletins painted the unique expression of our
relationship: two distinct forming one complete. We even stayed
up late one night gluing tiny bows and roses (which didn't want
to stick) onto our unity candle. It became an excellent exercise in
unity. I looked for a dress that would please my husband because I
wanted his heart to leap when he saw me. I wanted him to delight
in me.

I learned our wedding rituals aren't empty pomp; they each
have meaning. Much of that meaning is drawn from the desires of
our hearts, and the sanctity of marriage. If I'd remained engaged
to my first fiancé longer, I'm sure I would have found it in me to
plan all the details of our wedding, but I wouldn't have found
the same depth of meaning in them. I would have accomplished

much but missed that my preparations weren't obligations, they were celebrations.

I don't think that level of experience can be manufactured, but it can be fostered. Tethering my life, my future, and my being to my husband meant untangling any cords that could tie me to another in mind, spirit, or body. In choosing my husband, I was rejecting all others.

Likewise in my faith, God requires the same, and even greater, devotion. He requires it because He deserves it. We learn what this devotion looks like in Him, and in His devotion to us. As I've surrendered the things in this life I thought brought me, or would eventually bring me, the most joy, He's shown me their limitations. He's filled me with greater joy in Him instead, and this joy begets deeper devotion. The things I've held tightest, once released to Him, passed away or were reborn into something I enjoyed infinitely more as I enjoyed it now with Him. In untying myself from my own efforts to achieve joy, in rejecting substitutes, I tethered myself closer to the source of all true joy: my Creator, Savior, Sustainer, and Betrothed King.

Practically speaking, I'm talking about activities and ambitions relinquished, and relationships being dissolved or redefined. In my experience, these things work out organically. When I focus my devotion on pursuing my relationship with God, on reading His Word, and communing with Him in thought, word, and deed, He illuminates my substitutes. He also changes the way they taste on my tongue.

There is a parable in Matthew 22 about a wedding. In it, the great king hosts a wedding feast. Many are invited. When the day draws near, the invited are too busy with their affairs to attend. They're more concerned with the lives they're trying to build, and the joys they're trying to manufacture. So the king sends messengers to every dark, dank corner of the kingdom to bring in guests. As was the custom, the king provided robes for the guests to wear. In the parable, one guest spurns the provision of the king, insisting on wearing his own clothes instead. The king sees, and confronts him, and the guest stands before the king without excuse. The rebellious guest is removed and slated for execution, joining all those who declined the invitation.

Executions? Did that get harsh quickly?

If so, I think it's because God takes His kingdom seriously. He takes commitment seriously. He takes His Son's bride seriously. He takes love seriously, and so should we.

The robes provided in the parable are the same robes we will wear, and the provision cost God dearly. Jesus becoming man, the Infinite confined to the finite, living a holy life, the Sinless bearing our sins and dying, the Eternal Source of all life drinking death—even death on a cross—provided us with spotless white robes. He provided a way for us to be together, to be near Him, stainless despite our naturally stained condition. It came at great cost. Spurning His robes, His grace, is rejecting the God who bled to provide it. As for the executions, all life is bound by the breath of God, and so every form of death awaits apart from Him.

But oh, the celebration of union with Him! Greater than any party we'll experience here and now. I want to prepare for my next wedding in all joy. I want my Savior to see me standing all in white and delight in His bride. I want His heart to leap.

The dress makes it real. It also makes the wedding possible. God delights in our wedding. He secured photographers in every generation to capture our creation, journey, and His wooing and redeeming us. He taught us to honor our parents, including us in His timeline. He has written the course of our betrothal by our hand: two distinct operating as one complete. He set us apart, set our day apart, as special and unique to Him. He sent out the invitation; we share in sending out the invitation. He already removed the veil.

And He alone provides our wedding gowns. He takes our deeds and sews them up in His. As He put on flesh and became man—the greater inhabiting the lesser for love alone—so we put on His righteousness and become more like Him, the lesser becoming greater.

I don't know about you, but I'm excited for my next wedding.

"Rather, clothe yourselves with the Lord Jesus Christ, and do not think about how to gratify the desires of the flesh" (Romans 13:14 NIV).

"For all of you who were baptized into Christ have clothed yourselves with Christ" (Galatians 3:27 NASB).

> And from the throne came a voice that said,
>
> "Praise our God,
>
> all his servants,
>
> all who fear him,
>
> from the least to the greatest."
>
> Then I heard again what sounded like the shout of a vast crowd or the roar of mighty ocean waves or the crash of loud thunder:
>
> "Praise the LORD!
>
> For the Lord our God, the Almighty, reigns.
>
> Let us be glad and rejoice,
>
> and let us give honor to him.
>
> For the time has come for the wedding feast of the Lamb,
>
> and his bride has prepared herself.

She has been given the finest of pure white linen to wear."

For the fine linen represents the good deeds of God's holy people.

And the angel said to me, "Write this: Blessed are those who are invited to the wedding feast of the Lamb." And he added, "These are true words that come from God." (Revelation 19:5–9 NLT)

CHAPTER 8

The ABCs of It

Train up a child in the way he should go,
Even when he is old he will not depart from it.
—Proverbs 22:6 (NASB)

So I homeschool. I am a homeschooler. Sometimes saying that feels like I'm coming out of a closet or joining a twelve-step program. Hello. My name is Cinnamon. I am a homeschooler.

In fact, I'm a second-generation homeschooler. I never attended any form of organized school before college. I never owned a locker or rode a school bus. I never mitigated cliques as a child, so I'm not easily labeled now, nor do I label others with ease. Having a smaller world growing up led to my seeing a bigger world now. Many of the intangibles in life I cradle dearly and count most valuable are due in some part, or in entirety, to being homeschooled.

That being said, I want to make it clear I hold no ill thoughts to other educational institutions, be they public, private, or other. I don't know schools well enough to decry their faults. And while I don't know schools, I've known many teachers. What I have seen in them is genuine concern and enduring passion for their students. I have seen them selflessly give of their own time, hearts, and finances in the hope of benefitting at least one child per year. They pour themselves out for a sea of tender faces they know will change next year. They cannot follow their students through their academic careers to secure their investment. Teachers start over every year, often battling indifferent bureaucracies, and, most sadly, indifferent parents. Every year they begin the battle again. Every year they go back to the start. They love. They give. They serve. I think that's heroic. I don't think I could do what they do. I often shy away from calling myself a teacher (I usually use the term *instructor* instead) out of sheer respect.

Homeschooling is in many ways a far simpler process. I oversee the same students from pre-preschool up. I choose curriculum and modify, refine, or replace it based on each student's needs. Last school year, my eldest daughter (who is quick with math concepts but burns out under excessive repetition) went from enjoying math to hating it. In the middle of the school year, I called it. I scrapped the curriculum we were using and began testing others until we found her perfect fit. We scrambled to catch up a little, but she enjoys math again. Once again we have days that begin with her asking, "Mom, I feel like starting with math today. Is that cool?" Yes, it's cool. It's very cool.

During this crisis—we'll call it the great Curriculum Crash of 2015—I berated myself for waiting so long to make the change. Early in the year I saw signs of burnout taking shape. I watched her desire fade, her passion cool, and her indifference and frustration build. Early on I thought, *Next year, I'm changing the math curriculum. We'll try a different approach.* Next year was too long coming for her. I nearly exhausted one of the homeschooler's greatest commodities: willing and teachable students.

My husband, who is marvelously supportive, grew up in private schools. He was quick to remind me that most schools don't usually dump curriculums midschool year for the needs of one student. While I was bemoaning my response time, I missed the value inherent in my ability to switch at all. I forgot I'm blessed; I can modify my daughter's educational experience based on her learning style.

But this example isn't just meant to illustrate some of the values of homeschooling; it also illustrates some of the struggles that threaten derailment. As a mom, I want my child to have the best possible opportunities to grow and learn. I also feel inadequate. Too easily my instruction becomes centered on my fears.

Is she getting enough? Is she doing enough? Am I enough?

My worst instructing, and parenting too, for that matter, comes from my fear. I have to practice mastering it, in one shape or another, nearly every day. I have to remember that God Himself gave me my children, and instructed me to train them. God trusted me, and so should I.

I remind myself of the benefits and motivations in our unique approach. Every family is different, as is every child, so homeschooling exists in a colorful spectrum as varied as the individuals involved. I may not homeschool every child to his or her college and career choices, but right now I do have good reasons for what we do.

For starters, as a parent, my children get the best part of my day. They get me while I'm still in my best condition. (They also get me in my worst conditions.) They get me after that first cup of coffee, when I'm fresh and ready to face the day. This sounds small, but it's invaluable. Nearly all of the best conversations I've had as a parent happened somewhere in these hours.

I also have an immense opportunity to teach my children the value of lifelong learning. This week we discussed the theory of education. We discussed first the *Oxford Dictionary*'s definition of science: "the intellectual and practical activity encompassing the systematic study of the structure and behavior of the physical and natural world through observation and experiment." In short, science is first an activity, not simply a collection of data. Science is a method of study, of evaluation, of thought. Science is what we call the process of thought we use to better understand all we can see and quantify.

Education is broader, but is made of the same substance. Learning isn't about amassing a set of facts or information; it is a mental discipline with no true finish line. It is a method of living and thriving. It is a constant, lifelong pursuit and joy. The goal of education isn't a diploma; it's a lifetime of enrichment. It is, "the exercise of vital powers, along lines of excellence, in a life affording them scope."[1]

When I fall into the trap of fear, I am sliding into the mindset that there is one collection of data that I must somehow cram into my child's head. This isn't so. My calling isn't to teach my children what to think, but how to think for themselves. I'm not meant to spoon-feed them knowledge; I'm to teach them how to hold the spoon. In short, I'm not trying to teach them enough data to survive; I'm trying to teach them how to live life to the fullest of their potentials. C. S. Lewis once wrote that proper rewards are not simply tacked on the activity for which they're given, but they are the activity itself in consummation. How true these words are for the broad pursuit of learning, discovering, refining, and expanding your understanding. It is a million consummations giving way into the infinite.

And I'm blessed. I live in a nation that allows me to follow my conscience in these matters. I live in a society that accepts it freely. Homeschooling isn't the same beast it once was. As a child, when people found out I was homeschooled, they looked me over with a dubious eye, asking, "What's that?" Now, though I often expect the same reaction, I'm just as often met with commendations. The community has grown too, which brings fuller opportunities.

---

[1] This is an old phrase I've loved for many years. The clearest citation for it I can find is *Edith Hamilton, The Greek Way. W. W. Norton & Company, Inc., 1964*, in which the author refers to it as an old Greek definition of happiness.

I've said before there's no higher pursuit than building into immortal souls; this is especially true of the little souls God Himself grants us to steward. I may not know where the future of our education will take us, but I'm grateful to enjoy the journey.

CHAPTER 9

Chewing on the Meat

Above all else, guard your heart,
for everything you do flows from it.
—Proverbs 4:23 (NIV)

*T*his is the chapter where I talk about sin. I'm not in love with this chapter. I've seen God uproot some weighty sins from my heart. I like believing the sins that remain are the cute, harmless ones, or worse, sins I am somehow justified in retaining. I know I am justified *from* my sin, not to my sin, but my attitude doesn't always reflect my knowledge.

Likewise, I know there are no cute, harmless sins. Every sin, every idol of the heart, requires a blood sacrifice. If sin isn't entirely enclosed in the blood sacrifice of Jesus, it will exact the cost elsewhere. My unrepentant sin can still exact a price from me and from the lives of those around me. It will draw blood somewhere, as the sacrificial system in the Old Testament illuminates for us. The sins I've held onto have often been the open windows and doors havoc uses to sneak into my life. Praise God, because He has protected me still.

Scripture makes it clear we are all sinners. If we say we are not, we are lying, and the Truth is not in us. I've known sin is inherent to the human condition. In fact, I believed for years that it is my original condition, my most base self, in every sense of the word. My identity pivoted around my being born bad, and somehow, some day, in some mysterious way, God would make me something foreign, something brand new.

This is true, but I no longer believe it's the whole truth. Jesus is God's ambassador in a ministry of reconciliation. 2 Corinthians 5:19 (NLT) says, "For God was in Christ, reconciling the world to himself, no longer counting people's sins against them." The word *reconciliation* implies bringing what's been separated back together. Reconciliation is akin to restoration. If God came to elevate me from my most natural state to a new, higher existence, there must be a million words to describe that transcendence. He doesn't use those words; He uses the word *reconciliation*. As I think on that, my identity is pulled backward through all the murky waters of my life, right back into my mother's womb, where God formed me in the inward parts. I am fearfully and wonderfully made.

Let me be clear: I believe I was born a sinner. As David says, "Behold, I was brought forth in iniquity, and in sin my mother conceived me" (Psalm 51 NASB). I don't believe I've ever experienced one breath free from my willful sins and the presence and effect of sin. But I exist as one part of a whole; I am woven into humanity. My gross design is nearly as old as earth itself. So I'm drawn even further back, backward through the wars and kings, backward through the forming church in the New Testament, backward through the lineage of promise in the Old Testament, all the way to Genesis.

I see God bending to earth, forming humans from dust with His own perfect hands, and breathing His own breath of life into them. I see Him forming out of humans intimate, trustworthy companions. He proclaims them to be in His own image; humankind was good.

We were good once; we were designed to be. Sin, our invention, spread through humanity, bringing death and destruction with it, but we weren't *created* for sin. We weren't made for it. It isn't in our original design. Those in Christ have tasted it. God, in His supreme grace, is always excavating our true purpose, our true design, from the rubble of our sins. As I've grown closer to Him, I see my sins more acutely. They are always before me. As I've grown closer to Him, I've also experienced freedom from sins in ways I never thought possible. Those experiences clean out the engine of my soul, and the engine runs smoother. Those experiences are glimpses of the original design functioning as it was created to function.

I know I will never be free from sin, but as I've said, I have tasted deep freedom from sins. Those moments impress on me that I was made to be pleasing to God, and every displeasing moment, every sin, from Genesis to now, from my genesis to now, can be expunged in the work of Jesus Christ.

How does this work out practically?

For years I struggled with pornography. Yeah, I said pornography. I'm just diving right in here. As a child, I was molested. I think it embedded this idea that a woman's value was somehow based in her sexuality, or in the pleasure men took from her. I hated it. It didn't fit right in me. I wrestled with it in those dark, quiet, lone times, and I often lost, I'm ashamed to admit. I believed God called me to be something better than me, but I also believed my most basic existence was all mixed up in the type of distortion and pollution pornography, and all sexual sin, produces. I begged God to deliver me secretly, so no one ever knew. Eventually, I confessed my sin to my husband.

Alison Krauss helped lead me out of it. One day I was folding laundry in the TV room, listening to the radio through the television (oh, what an age we live in). A song by Alison Krauss came on, and a picture of the album cover appeared on the screen. She stood on a beach, I think. She dressed modestly, in a pale lace dress. I cannot say why it impacted me so deeply. She stood there motionless while her sweet voice played. I was taken with the purity of her voice, of her unique song in the world. She looked beautiful, wholesome.

In that moment, my view of women changed. I saw women are made to be helpmates, not playthings. God made us to be unique creations, not conforming recreations. We are made for dignity, integrity, and beauty. We are made to use our whole beings to glorify God, not our external frames to entertain men. In that moment, I broke into praise. In that moment, relying on Jesus to clean all that is past, I stepped into my most authentic identity: the woman He created me to be. When I saw the truth, the lie became hideous.

I've never looked back. In those dark, quiet, lone times, there is no pull anymore. I know what it is now, and it has no part with me. I pray I never go back to the lie. I remind myself of the truth daily, but not to avoid my past sins. I remind myself of the truth because it is the most beautiful expression of my existence I've ever known.

Pornography is, in its very essence, an enormous, horrific distortion. We call it a perversion, and well it is; it perverts a person's very cause of existence. It robs people of their callings, their gifts, and their design. It destroys all women's value everywhere. It is murder, stealing and destroying lives. I pray all who are touched by it run to the truth, cling to it, and find life and freedom. I pray for the day when the enslaved are set free. I pray for the day God does away with it once and for all.

There is a great mystery folded into my current understanding of sin. Just as God's original intent for us was good, our final condition will be infinitely better. In some mysterious way, as we are impacted by our original human condition, we share in our final one here too. If we are in Christ, we are a new creation.

"For we died and were buried with Christ by baptism. And just as Christ was raised from the dead by the glorious power of the Father, now we also may live new lives ... give yourselves completely to God, for you were dead, but now you have new life. So use your whole body as an instrument to do what is right for the glory of God" (Romans 6:4, 13 NLT). In Him we have died, and in His resurrection we share in His life. He designed us for good, and we rebelliously broke it, but our old design is reconciled to God in the death of Jesus, and our new lives begin in the power of His resurrection. We no longer regard each other according to the flesh anymore.

Jesus came as a human. Immanuel, God with us, came as a human. He lived sinless, but He bore our sin in His flesh. He walked among us, and those He walked with touched Him. They watched Him eat and sleep, and they knew He was human: flesh and bone. They also knew He was more. After His death and resurrection, He walked again with the same men, but they didn't recognize Him. He was changed. He still showed the scars from His life. He still ate and drank. He was still human, but in a way we didn't recognize.

But we will know it. We will be changed ourselves. In my struggle against sin, I remind myself that my life, from Genesis to Revelation, is tucked inside Christ's life. In Him my sin is not counted, and I somehow share in His new life. I am in metamorphosis, in the microcosm of my life, and in the macrocosm of the church through all time, in which I am a member: I was made to be good. I've chosen rebellion and aberration. I've appealed to Christ, who is transforming me. I will someday be changed into His glorious likeness, as it says in Philippians 3: "What a mystery; what a redemption!"

> And all of this is a gift from God, who brought us back to himself through Christ. And God has given us this task of reconciling people to him. For God

was in Christ, reconciling the world to himself, no longer counting people's sins against them. And he gave us this wonderful message of reconciliation. So we are Christ's ambassadors; God is making his appeal through us. We speak for Christ when we plead, "Come back to God!" For God made Christ, who never sinned, to be the offering for our sin, so that we could be made right with God through Christ. (2 Corinthians 5:18–21 NLT)

CHAPTER 10

Scuffing My Feet

Jesus said to him, "The one who has bathed does not
need to wash, except his feet, but is completely clean;
And you are clean, but not every one of you."
—John 13:10 (ESV)

oday is a hard day. Yesterday morning I wrote a chapter on
sin. I used an example of a sin from which God delivered me.
I got to spend the rest of the day seeing all the sin I still harbor—all
I want to do but don't and all I hate to do but do anyway. Yesterday
reminded me that to miss the mark at all means to fall profoundly
short.

Today I am reminded that I am already clean because of the
word He's spoken to me (John 15:3 NASB). I need to remember
it, because I don't feel it. I don't feel clean today. I feel like a sinful
mess. I've walked with God over three decades now, sometimes
fervently, and sometimes at a distance. He has always walked with
me in Spirit and in Truth. The longer we journey together through
this strange land, the holier He becomes.

Not to say for an instant that He is changing; He is the same yesterday, today, and forever, as it says in Hebrews 13:8. He is and always was and evermore shall be the thrice holy God: Holy, Holy, Holy.

I am not.

Jesus is the light of the world, and walking with the light involves exposure and awareness: a sudden ability to see what you could not see or would not see. Daniel praised God, saying, "It is He who reveals the profound and hidden things; He knows what is in darkness, and the light dwells with Him" (Daniel 2:22 NASB). In the light, our dark deeds are exposed; our sin finds us out.

And the scales just keep falling from my eyes. The longer I walk with God, the more I see His impeccable perfection and His acute beauty. The longer I walk with God, the higher I realize He is. The longer I walk with God, the more I see the depth and breadth of my sin. The longer I walk with God, the more I see my selfish ugliness and lowness. Yet the longer I walk with Him, the higher I become, because I better see more than just my sin.

I see the cross better too.

He poured out His death so I can be clean. He poured out His life so in the light, to Him, I am righteous. The only way I can bear to walk with Him in the light is to walk in light of the cross. The only way I can bear to face my sin, to really see it for what it is, is through the knowledge that my sin may be where I am right now but it isn't *who* I am.

I am His.

Our shoes show where we've been. I have four kids; trust me, I know. In our front foyer we have a shoe basket and a shoe shelf, but most of the shoes end up in a pile between the two. There is a near constant arrangement of shoes in every size, color, and style. We have a shoe for every purpose. We have a few shoes I'm convinced serve no real purpose.

I often sort through this congregation of shoes, and if there's one thing abundantly clear about them, it's that they reflect where the feet have been. Sometimes they're covered in mud or soaked through. Sometimes they've got mulch from the playground hitching a ride home, sometimes debris from the woods. I've seen them covered in sidewalk chalk, clumps of snow, and even ash from the uninterred remains of a bonfire.

Our feet rub against the earth wherever we tread. Our feet reflect the paths we travel. I can't help but bear that in mind when I read this verse about Jesus washing His disciples' feet. They're eating together when Jesus rises from the table, knowing His time is close, knowing He came from God and will soon return, and begins to wash their feet.

I imagine Peter looking at his own feet, at where he'd been in life, knowing in his heart Jesus had no business in that mess. And maybe Jesus didn't, but He had business with Peter, so He prepared to wash his feet. Peter cried out, "You shall never wash my feet!" He knew Jesus is King: holy, clean, and above all that is. Why would He kneel in humility to wash off whatever Peter had chosen to step in?

Why?

This is the heart of the question for me. Why would the Holy draw near to the repugnant? Why would the clean God apply His pure hands to filthy feet of flesh? I've found the clearest resounding answer for me a few verses earlier. It says, "Having loved His own who were in the world, He loved them to the end" (John 13:1 NASB). Jesus, knowing His time on earth was coming soon to an end, used every bit of that time to love His own.

Jesus answered, I imagine, as I would hope to respond to my child, in tender instruction. "If I do not wash you, you have no part with me." Peter responds, "Then wash not only my feet, but also my hands and my head." Jesus says, "He who has bathed needs only to wash his feet, but is completely clean; and you are clean" (John 13:8-10 NASB).

Herein is contained a great mystery of sanctification for me. Jesus looks at me through Himself, through His love and sacrifice, and I am already clean. I am bathed in His righteousness, His cleanness, His goodness. He sees me as clean, and yet, if I do not let Him wash my feet, I have no part with Him.

Yesterday was hard; my feet were dirty. In the light yesterday, I saw how filthy they'd become. I saw every dark path I've wandered on this foul earth, and all the filth I've stepped in. I didn't want God to wash it. I wanted to clean it myself. I wanted to cover some of it up without cleaning it at all. Some piles I've stepped in before, and I know I will step in again, and it's humiliating to bring the same messes back to God, again and again. It frustrates me that the standard is so high, so unattainable, as though if we all conceded to live in filth, the world would somehow be a better place.

But I know that just isn't so.

What I forget, faced with all my small humiliations, is the overwhelming humility of Jesus, the clean, kneeling to wash His creations' dirty feet. Before Jesus every knee shall bow, and yet He bowed first for us, to clean us in preparation because He loves us.

I forget where I've been is not who I am.

I am His.

I wish I lived in the childlike faith of my own children, who, after frolicking in muck, realize they need help getting clean. My sweet children, who cry out to me for help when they need it, because they know I love them, and I care for them. I hope I can always be the steadfast, loving parent to them that God has first been to us, who, having loved us, loves us to the end.

CHAPTER II

Rated R for Sexual Content

Kiss me and kiss me again,
for your love is sweeter than wine.
—Song of Solomon 1:2 (NLT)

*A*s I write this, I'm already thinking I won't include it in the book. I'm uncomfortable writing this chapter for several reasons: I'm actually kind of shy, and this topic is intensely personal. I'm not sure that anyone who might read this would be comfortable either. I'm not sure this isn't a topic that *should* stay personal, behind closed bedroom doors, or folded exclusively into the confidences of spousal pillow talk. One of my strongest reasons is that I'm not sure I have much to share that's helpful in any way; this is a weak area for me. I don't feel like I know enough or have any worthwhile experiences to relate.

I feel blind when it comes to sex. It's a topic you won't find me discussing in a church foyer on a Sunday afternoon, and I'd be far too embarrassed to ever consider making an appointment for it. Sometimes that strikes me as odd. Sex is everywhere and talked about by everyone. I don't need to tell you our culture is saturated; we all know it is. Still, I find the subject not only personal to me but also uniquely personal to me and my husband as a couple. Our sex life is an intimate reflection of each of us as individuals and both of us as one.

But nonetheless, here goes.

As I've mentioned earlier, I was molested as a child. It continued for most—nearly all—of my childhood. Its presence exists in some of my earliest memories. Misuse of that nature usually skews wholesome development. By the time I came of age, I'd learned hundreds of lessons about sex, none of them valuable to my marriage as far as I can tell. In my abuse, I was exposed to pornography, which you now know developed its own gravity for me later in my adulthood. Sex was never about pleasure for me; it was about survival and identity.

I share all of this to say that I didn't begin my adult life with a surplus of wisdom in this area. I didn't even start at zero. I started in the negatives. I started *way* in the negatives.

I'm not sure where I am now.

Here is where I began.

In my teen years, my youth group preached a lot about sexual purity pleasing God and protecting your life. That was hard for me. I felt distraught that I'd never in my memory been sexually pure. I still hadn't told anyone of the molestation, and so no one had yet told me it wasn't my fault. Even if they had, it might not have changed the substance of it. In my understanding of purity, causality factored in very little. A thing was pure or it was tainted, and I was tainted.

If you're reading this now, and you share similar life experiences, know that it wasn't your fault. Neither the abuse nor the complex sins that grow out of it will ever deter the love of Jesus from finding you and from proclaiming you clean. He flocks to the broken; He gathers them under His wing like a mother hen. You are pure in Him, and nothing on earth or in heaven, in your past, your present, or your future—no power that exists in any realm—can ever separate you from His love. You are loved for who you are by the One who made you.

In my youth, I responded by taking the "True Love Waits" commitment. I promised to stay pure until I entered into a covenant marriage relationship. I meant it. I also never intended to get married, but in my early twenties I found myself in a relationship, somewhat by accident. Then he proposed, and I promised to marry him. Sexually speaking, things went well for a while. He knew I vowed to wait, and he seemed to respect that. Then one day his father pulled him aside. He told his son not to pressure me to have sex, because I'd give in to him.

As he related his conversation to me, it horrified me. I recognized truth in all that his father said to him, but what most bothered me was how well his father seemed to know me, and how little he must have known his own son. After that, sex became a big deal between us. I did give in, for a plethora of reasons, but none of them were good reasons. In time, my fiancé grew to hate me. The relationship didn't end well.

I felt broken, insufficient, and betrayed (as much by myself as my fiancé). I emptied myself for him of everything I held most dear, most valuable, and he seemed to hate me all the more for it; just as well, I think I hated myself too.

Sex is powerful. We treat it like a primal need, a mere bodily function, but it is far more. Sex can nurture love or foster hate. Sex can weave two souls together into one, or it can rip two woven souls apart; it can tear a soul apart. Sex can change a person's self-identity. Sex can drive people into slavery, into usury, into addiction, into poverty, into wealth, and into murder.

I was friends with my now-husband while engaged, and we began our relationship a month after my engagement ended. I wish I could say my prior relationship didn't deeply impact my relationship with my husband. I cannot. As recently as last night I discussed insecurities still embedded in me from that experience. When I began dating my husband, I considered "good sex" as job security—nothing more, nothing less.

My husband was wiser than I was, and more resistant. After we married, I began to see my understanding in this area fell tragically short. I searched scripture for marital advice and found 1 Corinthians 7. It says husbands and wives should stop depriving each other. Their bodies belong to each other. I purposed in my heart to never turn my husband down for sex.

Of course, I didn't tell him that. I was scared he would think I was only sleeping with him out of obligation, or worse, that he'd take advantage. I didn't yet understand trust as a key component to good sex. I always assumed one day I'd break my purpose, but I didn't. I've still never turned him down. He made that possible by treating me with respect.

Here is what I gained by sharing my body with him.

After I had my first daughter, my body changed. I felt unattractive. I didn't feel like having sex. As I mentioned earlier, I felt alone in our marriage, so I didn't feel like sleeping with him, but I did. I often prayed in my heart during our intercourse. I prayed I would want him. I prayed he would enjoy me. I prayed God would be pleased by us. I prayed I would love my husband in a way God esteems. What started with hesitancy usually ended in joy.

In practicing loving my husband when I didn't feel "in the mood," I started seeing sex as something more than sating an appetite. I saw it as something other than job security. It was an intimate mystery, sometimes a salve, and it opened my heart to him. In practicing loving him with my body regardless of my momentary preferences, my lifelong preference grew into him alone. I learned to see beyond myself, to see him, and practice putting him first. By not withholding even my own flesh, by not keeping my needs and desires separate from his needs and desires, he became uniquely mine: my one, my mate, my confidant and closest friend.

Last night I was sitting on my porch when a neighbor walked by. He poured his soul out to me, and it was broken. His marriage might be over. He and his wife considered sex no more than a bodily function; they shared their marriage bed. They were both adults, he said, and he assumed he'd be fine with it, but he isn't. They're not in love anymore, so why even try to make it work?

I think sex might be designed to reflect the unity of God in one of the most mysterious parts of His existence: three as one. In sex, two become one. I think it's possible, in God-centered marital sex, that He indwells it too: three as one. When we invite others into our sexual thoughts or practices, or when we shut our spouse out of them, I think we turn the purpose of sex against itself. What unites in a powerful, mysterious way can also destroy with the same fervor.

Last night I talked about some of these things with my husband. I talked about my failures in this area and also my hopes. Our emotional and spiritual intimacy gave way to physical intimacy, which gave way to joy.

> Love is patient, love is kind and is not jealous; love does not brag and is not arrogant, does not act unbecomingly; it does not seek its own, is not provoked, does not take into account a wrong suffered, does not rejoice in unrighteousness, but rejoices with the truth; bears all things, believes all things, hopes all things, endures all things. Love never fails. (1 Corinthians 13:4–8 NASB)

CHAPTER 12

Vapors and Vespers

The conclusion, when all has been heard, is: fear God
and keep His commandments,
because this applies to every person.
—Ecclesiastes 12:13 (NASB)

Sometimes I feel an impression of meaningless rambling in life, a random collision of events. A selfish man may die an old tycoon, leaving behind a string of ex-wives still in their youth, while an honorable man's life is cut short, leaving behind the beloved wife of his youth. Some infants are abandoned, abused, or neglected, while others are pulled from the outstretched arms of loving families by death or circumstance; grief is tasted, and an endless ache takes residence in the soul. There are turf wars, holy wars, massacres, genocide, euthanasia, and abortion. There is racial injustice, gender inequality, a caste system, and socioeconomic oppression. Children in one country die from diseases another country vaccinates against at no charge. Children die at all.

We have a theory called "the lottery of birth." Many of us recognize what distinguishes our efforts from others can often be reduced to a flick of chance. Had we been born in a different time, a different country, or a different skin, all we think is so unique to our personal identities may very well have grown in a different direction. Many more seem to live in the adamant assumption that all they've achieved is due solely to their own efforts, as though their stories are disconnected from all others, disconnected from their own causality. They affirm or acknowledge no benefit from birth or breeding.

But we don't exist in a vacuum. The timeline of humankind is more than history; it's momentum. Everyone on earth has a story, a brief ignition, burn, and fade, and the energy converted moves on through us all. It feels like we're all entangled, from the dawn of humankind to the final birth. Humanity, through all space-time, moves like one organism. Each cell is of similar substance within a spectrum of purposes. Some benefit the organism; some do not. The organism itself is capable of great beauty, great compassion, and great achievement, but also great horror, great indifference, great cruelty, and great destruction. As we've learned the function of the human body in stages through the ages, so do we have an opportunity to glimpse the function of the body of humanity.

We are made to mirror our Creator. In our self-determination, we bring our highest wisdoms into tangible realities. In our art, our music, our words, our engineering, our ingenuity, and our every expression of constructive activity, we reflect back God our Creator. We search the deep, the distant, and the infinitesimal for order and meaning. We look to see His fingerprints.

In our destruction, our avarice, and our cold indifference to our own organism, we show the natural course of all that rebels from His design. We give occasion for Him to showplace His fearsome wrath and awesome power. Sometimes He moves, and the earth trembles. Sometimes He waits in wisdom and long-suffering patience for the final redemption of the design of humankind.

And it's too immense for me. I'm so small. I'm such a tiny

flash—half-burned, half-faded, and still guessing at my own purpose, my own telos. Some days I struggle against a current to find meaning in meaninglessness, to find order in chaos. I struggle to believe that in the ocean of variables, the teeming sea of the manifold into which I'm tossed by birth, my decisions matter; my small cell affects the great organism. I strain my eyes to see over the choppy waves of incident and doubt.

But other days, cause and effect are palpable. Today has been idyllic. In the morning, I took the kids to the park. The older three played in the warm, inviting sun while I sat by my sleeping infant with a cool drink, a pen, and blank, inviting paper. As my children laughed, running from play set to play set, I looked back on my life—all the decisions that brought me to today. I saw the applied wisdom God granted me in warm kindness, and it manifested in flesh. If I spurned His insight at key points in my life, reacting as my emotions dictated over what I knew was right, I wouldn't still be married. Two of these beautiful children wouldn't exist. This day in history wouldn't be here; it would have swerved off the course, leading me to an emptier day where two exquisite souls never came into being.

Today I'm eating the fruit of good decisions, and the fruit is good, bringing health to my bones. My infant never once cried today. She giggled at the cool breezes coming in playful spurts. I sat in the shade of the picnic table while my children worked on math and phonics, and I tried to impart some morsel of the wisdom that brings good life, good fruit, to its hearers.

Yet if you asked me what brought this moment into being, my answer would be providence. My children were born alive and thriving. My husband and I live, and he also stayed committed to me when more appealing routes forked in front of him. A relationship that began in shallow foolishness and blindness has been given time and the environment needed to grow roots. God placed in my life the good counsel of wise friends, who steered me back onto the path of life when I began to swerve. We have, thus far, been spared from sudden tragedy. Even today, this seventy-seven-degree day, warm on the skin and kissed by a cool breeze, is a mid-February surprise. Wisdom brought me here, and also the finger of God stirring the variables I call chance.

And I am not alone. We eat the fruit of our decisions, but we also partake in the fruit of the organism at large. We contend with the natural world, humankind's encompassing ecosystem into which we introduced imbalance and malady. And the creation groans, looking forward to being made whole again, waiting to yield its fruit, and restless to see its returns. We eat also of the providence of God, who causes the rain to fall on the righteous and the unrighteous.

I call these variables chance because I cannot calculate them for their sheer magnitude. I call life random because I cannot devise a formula to accommodate all of its intricacies or to predict its next movement. I call life chaos because it is a splayed mass of blood and bone and skin.

But so is an operating table. If I looked into a person's gut with my untrained eye, I couldn't distinguish between each layer in the blood. I couldn't see what is intact and what is wounded, what should be sutured or what should be cut. I couldn't, but the alert eye of the trained surgeon can, with ease. When I cry, "Chaos! Chance! Meaninglessness!" there is one variable for which I have not accounted: the skilled transcendence of the Great Architect.

God didn't toil over creation; He spoke. Everything came to be in His order, to His specifications. He knew every moment ahead, and He laid the foundation of the world accordingly. He fashioned humans in two parts: the dust of earth and the Breath of the Eternal. He gave humans good activity and good fruit with which to take and eat their fill. He gave humans gulps from His own deep well of wisdom, the path to a good life, and caution against the folly that pounces to destroy. He built evidences for humans to trace and provisions to sustain them, and wonder to call forth praise, into the original design. There is no chaos in His reign.

He formed humans, the lineage of mankind, the great organism, to survive the cancer of sin. God Almighty, the Great Physician, sees us laid open before Him. Our lives are open books to Him. He is intimately familiar with every layer of our being; He sees the entire organism at once. Our complexity is simplicity under His scalpel. He has not rejected us in our destruction; He has not forsaken us in our myopic despair. He, God Transcendent, God Self-Existent, God the Just, God the Wise, God the Good, God the Powerful, God the Holy, Holy, Holy, is ever God with Us.

CHAPTER 13

The Heart of the Matter

When I consider Your heavens, the work of Your
fingers,
The moon and the stars, which You have ordained;
What is man that You take thought of him,
And the son of man that You care for him?
—Psalm 8:3–4 (NASB)

*D*o me a favor; close your eyes and picture lying on your back in a vast field stretching out endlessly in every direction. Feel the lush grass beneath you. Now look into the black canopy of night sky above you, and picture every star blazing. See them all, the brilliant, burning beacons piercing the dark with bright, pure light. Some burn large and bright, others twinkle small and dim. Some group in clusters like a heavenly choir, while others stand as lone sentinels in luminescent strength. Some are ancient elders, fixtures of praise. Some are newly forming. Some fall, streaking the sky with a sudden stroke painted in light and holy flame.

It's hard to look at just one, isn't it? They sing together, one tapestry, one masterpiece, one immense family lifting praise to the Creator. The black sky threatens to cover us in darkness, in separation, in blindness, and in fear, but God's light pierces through it in a million different points of light to remind us He is God and has overcome the darkness. All those brilliant stars lift up one congregation of witness. We are awed. We are touched by the impression we have seen the works of God.

As I write this, I sit under a night sky. The stars are fading, yielding the dance floor to the upcoming king of the sky, the fierce sun, into which no humans gaze but at their own peril. Like so many generations before me, I am touched by the wonder of these celestial beings. I am touched by the wisdom of God, painting proof of His activity, His methods, and His immutable power and insight, across all creation. We are without excuse. I am without excuse. But when the sun comes, I stop staring. My eyes fall to earth. My ambitions fall to the ground around me. My wonder falls asleep, and I strive with lesser things. How peculiar that in the light of the greatest star, I forget wonder. How peculiar that the more I see, the less I gaze.

Perhaps that's because the more I see, the more muck I see. When I came to sit here in the dark, I only saw the vague impression of things. I saw the muted frame of my chair, my little table, and the railing running beside. In the light, I see cracks in the chair and bits of leaves and rings from coffee mugs gone by on the table. I see corners and crevices of dirt and cobwebs on the railing. What appeared clean by starlight is shown in true condition by sunlight.

Today I bear my sin in mind as I ponder God's holiness and glory. In the Bible, God's glory is spoken of as fire and smoke; His holiness burns pure and untamable. His eyes are too pure to approve evil; He cannot look on wickedness in favor, as stated in Habakkuk 1. By His holiness, men died.

I'm drawn to the story in 2 Samuel of David bringing home the ark of the covenant. The ark represented the very throne of God: the Holy, Fearsome, Ancient of Days. God Himself gave special instruction for moving the ark: the priest alone approached it, covered it, and a family He set aside for the task carried it by poles on their shoulders. David, a man after God's own heart, instead gathered all the choice men of Israel and bought a brand new cart. He employed every kind of musician for the procession, and he, King David himself, was chief in attendance. Any person on earth would be honored by this wild parade thrown in his or her honor.

But God is not man.

In the height of revelry, the oxen stumbled. Their beastly legs threatened to upset the cart. For one moment, the symbol of the very presence of God became relegated to the practical concern of stumbling to the ground, and Uzzah, a man probably not allowed to carry the ark on his shoulder, took hold of it with his hand. For one moment, the power of God appeared to be supported by the hand of a man. And God's anger burned at his irreverence. He killed Uzzah where he stood.

David was angry with God, and was unwilling to bring the ark of the Lord home that day. I wonder if David assumed, as I often do, that his enthusiasm would cover a multitude of sins. It seems to me, instead of worshiping God in the humility of obedient submission, David also showcased his own glory too. He displayed publicly all the glory God bestowed on him through his chosen men, choice musicians, his victories and position, and even his own song and dance.

I'm cut to the quick. If even David, having walked with God as a shepherd and runt of his own litter, having slain Goliath and countless Philistines by trusting in the power of God, having submitted to a wicked king bent on destroying his God-given ordainment out of reverence alone for Saul's God-given position, if even this David could be vulnerable to this great sin, how much more so am I?

Nothing I am, nothing I do, is bound solely for God's glory. I take selfish allowances and make fleshly concessions. I act like my intentions justify my failings, but too often my intentions aren't to serve God; my intentions are to impress Him.

The sun rises. By the light, I see the muck in my heart. Sin is common to humankind; it is ordinary and expected. I don't see it as it is because I don't want to. "The heart is deceitful above all things, and desperately wicked; who can know it?" (Jeremiah 17:9 KJV). God knows it. When God called David in from the fields, He warned Samuel not to judge by appearances, "for God sees not as man sees ... the Lord looks at the heart" (1 Samuel 16 NASB).

If you're still with me, I ask you to close your eyes one more time and picture the garden of Eden. Picture the luxurious, abundantly fruitful, safe environment of the thriving garden. Picture Adam and Eve, in all their splendor, enjoying paradise with unbreakable bodies. Imagine their joyful companionship, unbroken and unburdened. Hear their laughter babbling like a running spring into each other's ears. Linger here, where creation walks in tune with Creator, and there has been no recorded death in all existence. Both day and night are equals. Adam and Eve are equals. Every day is pleasant and fulfilling.

Now picture the idea forming in Adam's mind that he could be a creature separate from his maker. He, made in the likeness of God, could be like God also in substance and power: independent. Perhaps, for a moment, he even thought he could impress God. Imagine him putting that idea to his lips to ingest it, but as the saliva of his rebellion mixes with the fruit of his disobedience, the first parasite forms: sin. Picture that crawling, teeming parasite streaming forth like an advancing sea of consuming ants, filling his mouth, and expanding to cover their bodies in writhing, black death. Picture those parasites burrowing into their once unbroken flesh, attacking their functions, and laying eggs. Picture them moving out like locusts over every tree and blade of grass, over every bird and beast, attacking and consuming their perfection while undermining their functions. In moments, nothing is spared. In moments, creation goes from pure, unbroken life, to crippled, teeming death.

And the Holy Creator sees all He made as good covered and

filled with parasite and maggot. The Holy, Holy, Holy Creator watches as humans create sin, and the rot and decay of it already stinks in His nostrils. The King of Life watches as humans commit treason, calling forth death. Adam and Eve don't see it, not yet, but the pure eyes of God do. His hatred for it burns, and He has ample power to crush it from existence and to blot it from the record, but to do so would mean crushing humans.

He chooses instead a harder way—one that requires intense forbearance, unfailing devotion, and, eventually, death by the painful consumption of the parasite of sin. In that moment, and every moment before and after, He chooses to drink that cup for our redemption, and for His glory.

There was a time that I saw God's hatred of sin as a preference. I can't see sin as God sees it. I only see a few of my sins at a time. I don't recline, like I do with the stars, and try to take them all in at once. Even if I could see all my sins, which I will never be able to do, I couldn't see all the sins of humankind through all the timeline of mankind. I'm incapable of seeing the birth of every sin, or the filth, pollution, perversion, and destruction they wreak on the organism of humankind. Even if I could, I'm incapable of being *other*, being separate, or being holy.

When God called David, He looked into the sin-riddled heart of a shepherd and saw the heart of a king. He sees our hideous sin, but He also sees the expression of humanity He created us to be. In His patience and in His love, He provided for us a way, through Himself, to one day be free from all the destruction we've wrought. By the ever-present power of His Spirit, through the spilled blood of His Son, He is applying the cure.

That is why, with a broken and contrite heart, we eagerly bow the knee to render praise where praise is due. That is why, in the face of my sin and failure, I sing.

"Then you will shine among them like stars in the sky as you hold firmly to the word of life" (Philippians 2:15b-16a NIV).

CHAPTER 14

All Good Things ...

> There is no fear in love; but perfect love casts out
> fear,
> because fear involves punishment,
> and the one who fears is not perfected in love.
> —1 John 4:18 (NASB)

*T*his little book was born out of one of my many failures. A month ago, I was in a dark, difficult place. I'd just given my testimony at church. While God powerfully upheld me and carried me through, the process brought back painful memories and clashes in my identity. It illuminated areas in which I still live in fear or faithlessness. The night I gave my testimony, I drove to my sister's house, and in my weakness, chose to start smoking again.

At the time I believed it was just for that night. Then it was just for that weekend. When I returned home, I still found it difficult to put them away. One night, I smoked the last cigarette in the pack and said goodbye to smoking. It'd been a fun tryst and an easy companion, but it was time to return to life as usual. Only the next day, I felt miserable. I'd underestimated the draw of it and overestimated my willpower. I couldn't sit still as minutes passed like hours, and my desire to smoke grew disproportionately larger than any reason I had to stop.

In near desperation, I e-mailed two friends. One of them supported me through the writing and delivery of my testimony. She still had no idea I'd started smoking at all. My letter was short. In it, I confessed to smoking and told her I was trying to quit, but I didn't want to. I loved smoking. I missed smoking. I didn't understand why I wasn't smoking right now.

I tried to wait for their responses, constantly checking my inbox, but I broke quickly. I halted the day's activities, packed the girls into the van, drove to the gas station, and bought a pack of Marlboro Reds.

I came home and put the younger ones to their naptime. I settled the older ones back in their work. Then I sneaked outside and smoked. With the thick eddies of relief came swirls of self-directed frustration, disappointment, and failure. I came back inside and checked my e-mail; my friend's response sat unopened in my inbox.

My heart sank. I braced myself for the confident encouragement that I could do all things, or the gentle reprieve not to lose ground after the breakthrough of my testimony, or shock I smoked at all. I braced myself to feel like a failure.

She didn't mention the smoking at all. She just laughed and said I should write a book about the full-time job of raising children and homeschooling in today's wacky world. I couldn't help but smile. I brought to her this momentous failure, and she was most poised to bear it against me, but her scope exceeded mine. She wasn't bound by my failure; she was looking to my design. I decided to write this book in that moment, hoping to give her the surprise smile she gave me that day.

Over the last two weeks, while writing this book, I have experienced breakthroughs in my faith. God has used the writing of it to lift my scope, my vision, off trying to impress Him, off of my failures, off the lies of my past, and onto the truth of what He has already accomplished. He used these words, and His Word, to bring me out of that darkness into His wonderful light. He shifted my gaze from the troubles of my past to the promise of my future in Him.

For the past twenty years, I have been a lover of the band Switchfoot. They're not my usual style; I swoon for the crooners and Louis Armstrong, Johnny Cash, and Chopin but not often for rock bands. Their lyrics stole my heart. Their songs mirrored my own strivings to dig deeper, to engage with the great mysteries of life, to embrace being human in all its complex facets, and to praise the knowable God of the Unknown. Their YouVersion video devotional has been the only one to date I've repeated. In the final day's video, Jon Foreman, the lead singer, talks about "hitting the wrong notes."

We are to let the music begin, as the prior day's psalm says, to dance and sing, for the Eternal is listening and nothing pleases Him more than His people. He points out what everyone who attempts to create cannot avoid: flaws are inherent to the struggle. Even in the best of me lurks the worst of me, causing dissonance and missteps, but our failures don't hinder God from creating through us. They don't hinder God from delighting in us. In the final day's video, Foreman reminds us of Psalm 103, saying God knows how we are formed. He remembers that we are dust. He knows we are dust, but we please Him.

I'll be honest; it's a struggle to picture the God of all perfection delighting in me. I am so far from any form or semblance of perfection.

But there are moments I can see Him better than I do now.

Before coming out to write this final chapter, I sat with my two-year-old. We bounced a balloon around. I read short portions of her board books to her, until her attention diverted. We played with her sorting cube, and I tried to entice her to name the shapes and colors. Every time I said, "Which one's blue?" or "Where's the oval?" I wasn't angry when she got it wrong. I'm not training her to complete job functions; she is not my equal (yet). Her ability to complete my requests matters solely because *she matters to me.* I'm not disappointed when she gets it wrong because it's not about what she accomplishes; it's about who she becomes. I care more about her than her accomplishments. I care more about her than her knowledge. I care more about her than her abilities. I'm not upset when she falls, but I rejoice when she takes her first steps. I'm not upset when she babbles, but I laugh out loud with her first words. Her failings don't interrupt the excitement of watching her stumble into every new skill. I delight in watching her grow.

If I, a sinful, flawed parent, can love my child this way, how much more does my heavenly Father delight in me? How much more does He delight in my naming the colors and shapes of this world, as best I can, even though I'm sure to get some wrong?

Afterword

He has shown you, O mortal, what is good.
And what does the LORD require of you?
To act justly and to love mercy and to walk humbly
with your God.
—Micah 6:8 (NIV)

*I*t's been a couple of weeks since I finished writing this book. After I finished it, I quit smoking, sent it to a few of my closest friends, and wrestled with the idea of publishing again. I missed writing, so I began writing new chapters. As I began typing them up, I got sick. I decided against adding them. I decided this book is tiny, but it's complete.

It's after midnight here. I'd just fallen asleep when a single thought woke me. I knew I needed to add it.

I talk a lot about design, purpose, and function. My brain works that way. Whenever I encounter a new system, I (often unintentionally) seek to learn its concepts and constructs and to understand all its moving parts and their purpose. It's never to exploit the system, or alter it, but just to understand it. I care about design, and function, and purpose, but not as ends in themselves. I care about them because they're imprints of their maker. To glimpse the purpose of an original design is to glimpse the intentions of the designer. To glimpse the intentions of a designer is to glimpse the designer's heart.

Last night, my husband and I talked about my design before we fell asleep. We talked about how writing is a visible extension of my thought process. It was all born from trauma. I grew up in an abusive environment that shattered the standard functions of my cognitive capabilities. It slivered my memory into vivid, untethered fragments. It shuffled my chronology. I've spent most of my life trying to rebuild the system. I've spent most of my active time working the moving pieces roughly into place based on every clue I can garner, always trying to understand where they go, why they fit, how they move, and what they mean. It's become a part of who I am now. I love puzzles. I love nearly every kind of puzzle. They aren't effortless. I have to really stretch my mental muscles, but what a fantastic opportunity as a human being on earth. We can comprehend the pieces and piece together the whole.

I think the things that bring me the deepest fulfillment now were born from the things that once caused my deepest rifts. Life itself looks like a puzzle, but it isn't. It's a working system. Life is a vast, complex, functioning paradox. It's full of seemingly contradictory parts, but in their proper place, everything fits. Every part functions. Every part reveals an aspect of the system. In the great coding of the universe, there lurks a subset, a diminishing virus if you want, but the code runs. The Great Architect has already put an end to the virus, even as it runs the rest of its limited course. The virus isn't capable of defeating the system. The system belongs to its Architect, and He is too patient and too clever to allow the system to fail. Even this, while true, is a gross simplification.

The system is vaster than the universe and more complex than a human body. It's big, I tell you, and polluted right now, but it's still beautiful. It's in the process of becoming something vaster, something more complex, but also simplistic, without the paradoxes of sin and grace, rebellion and patience and justice. Perfect function, without hatred, fear, cruelty, greed, abandonment, isolation, abuse, divorce, or death, is the original design; the beauty of the original design reflects its Designer. The system is being purified, and when all is heard, it will function flawlessly, impervious to any future assault. It's fighting disease now, but it will be immune to disease when it's done. We share in His grace, in His inclusion, and even in His working within the system now. We are His hands and feet, and the work is great. I love it.

God made me by design, too, with a function, and for a purpose. The closer I operate as He intended, the smoother runs the engine of my soul. I am being purified. This day will run its course, and He will restore me to the beauty of His intent. What He does in us, in our microcosms, He is doing through all the timeline of humankind, our macrocosm.

But all of this is *how* life functions.

The greatest, most profound mystery isn't in the paradox of our current form of existence. That is, to some extent, conceivable. We can see; we can reason; we can reach for it.

The greatest, most profound mystery isn't in the *how* but in the inconceivable *why*.

Why did He make me?

Why did He make you?

Why did He make water to form clouds in the sky, and ocean tides, and tears of joy? Why did He make trees to provide heat, art, beauty, structure, and life? Why did He form flowers to briefly bloom as single, fragile, vivid masterpieces?

Because it pleases Him.

This is the thought that woke me.

Because it pleases Him.

My husband and I will soon celebrate twelve years of marriage. In the last twelve years, we've hurt each other deeply. We've made each other angry. We've disappointed each other. We've grown closer. We've worked on our communication and on our commitment. We've shared life, intimately. I've tried to follow his lead, and he's never pulled rank on me. His love isn't required; it is a gift he gives me every day.

This is the *how*, but the *why*?

We are married because we want to be. We value our commitment. We consider the sum of our marriage to be greater than the parts. We are married because we love each other. We desire each other's presence. We seek the other's fulfillment. I seek my husband because I love him, and he loves me. Love, sturdy love, in all its complex facets, is our *why*.

I seek to obey God not to fulfill a utilitarian function but to make Him smile. He loves me in the face of all I've done to hurt Him, to make Him angry, or to disappoint Him. He loves me beyond all that. We grow closer.

I exist because He smiles at my existence. Because He smiles, I eagerly look for ways to make Him smile all the more. He was never required to love me the way He does; it is a gift He gives me every day. His enduring, enthusiastic love draws a response from my depths, even as I struggle to see it, to believe it, and to embrace it. His love restores me, changes me, purifies me, and quickens me. Because He loves me, I want to follow Him along the path of life. I want to seek Him first. I want to lay down my life for Him. Because He loves me, I want to love Him; I want to obey Him. I want to be more like Him.

He is just; may I ever act justly.

He is merciful; may I ever love mercy.

He is God Almighty, the Maker of heaven and earth, the Ancient of Days, the Sinless Lamb, the Sacrificial Savior, the Fearsome Judge, Wisdom and Goodness and Justice and Love, the Waymaker.

He is God With Us. May I ever walk humbly with Him.

Printed in the United States
By Bookmasters